STEPHEN THRAVES COMPACT ADVENTURE GAME BOOKS

ASSIGNMENT LOCH NESS

Illustrated by Peter Dennis

HODDER AND STOUGHTON
LONDON SYDNEY AUCKLAND

British Library Cataloguing in Publication Data

A catalogue record for this book is available from the British Library

ISBN 0 340 58862 4

Text copyright © Stephen Thraves 1993
Concept copyright © Stephen Thraves 1993
Format copyright © Stephen Thraves 1993
Illustrations copyright © Peter Dennis 1993

First published 1993

The rights of Stephen Thraves to be identified as the author of the text of this work and of Peter Dennis to be identified as the illustrator of this work have been asserted by them in accordance with the Copyright, Designs and Patents Act 1988.

Published by Hodder and Stoughton Children's Books,
a division of Hodder and Stoughton Ltd,
Mill Road, Dunton Green, Sevenoaks, Kent TN13 2YA

Photoset by Rowland Phototypesetting Ltd,
Bury St Edmunds, Suffolk

Printed in Great Britain by Biddles Ltd,
Guildford and King's Lynn

All rights reserved

COMPACTS are very different from every other type of adventure game book. They have been specially designed so that their play is as convenient as possible.

Your score cards are on special fold-out flaps, so your current score will always be there at a glance. These flaps also contain all your *adventure accessories*. The only thing you have to provide yourself is a pen or pencil to mark your score card.

You don't even need an eraser because there are enough score cards (a whole 40!) to allow for a fresh one to be used for each new game.

COMPACTS are ideal for playing at home, on holiday, in the car . . . wherever you like!

◇ THE ASSIGNMENT ◇

'In my office!' the editor barks as his door suddenly flies open and he stands there with his finger pointing intimidatingly at you. 'At once!'

All the other people in the room go silent, word processors freezing mid-line, as you rise nervously to your feet. There are stares all around. *What have you done?* Is this the sack? Is this the end of your photo-journalism career already? This newspaper is your very first job – and you've only been here two days!

'Don't bother to sit down,' your fearsome editor snaps as you quake before him. 'There isn't time. We've got an emergency on. All our regular photographers are out covering other stories at the moment – and so we're going to have to send YOU on the assignment. Eight sightings in just one day! And all from reliable witnesses, according to the morning news. What a time to have only a junior photographer available!'

You are confused. 'Sightings of what, sir?' you ask.

'Of the Loch Ness monster, of course!' he bellows at you. 'Not a glimpse for years – not even a ripple on the water – and now eight clear sightings at once, all round the north end of the loch. We've got to get the photographs before any of the other newspapers do. I want them in our very next issue. Or it might well be our last.'

'What do you mean?' you ask with concern. Was the newspaper doing badly? Was it about to fold? Perhaps your first job wasn't the wonderful opportunity it had appeared.

'What I mean,' he spells out brusquely, 'is that if those other newspapers beat us to it once again, we're finished. They're doing it every single time and pinching all our readers. We must be FIRST with this one. It would be the greatest scoop of them all!'

You jump as he suddenly thumps his fist on his desk. 'Now, what are you waiting for? Have a quick look at the video of that news item and then get yourself on the very next plane to Inverness. I must have those photographs ready for the next issue's deadline. That's no later than eleven o'clock tonight.'

Eleven o'clock tonight! you keep repeating to yourself with alarm as you hurriedly pack all your cameras into a shoulder bag, then jump into a taxi for the airport. That's only thirteen hours away! Just thirteen hours to fly up to Inverness, travel the dozen or so miles to the loch, take the photographs, and then fly all the way back again!

And that's if the monster is being co-operative. What if it's being elusive?

But imagine if you *do* manage to snap it, you think with a smile as you catch the plane just in time. Not only will you save your newspaper but you'll surely become their star photographer overnight.

You're still day-dreaming as you arrive at Inverness airport and jump into a mini-cab that suddenly appears at the taxi queue.

At least, you're *told* that it's a mini-cab by the driver before he puts your camera bag into the boot. But as you're travelling to the loch you become suspicious.

Firstly, who's that silent blonde woman, sitting next to the driver? Secondly, aren't those bags of theirs near your feet *also* camera bags? And how is it that they've got flight tags on them? Could it be that the couple have only just landed at Iverness themselves, this merely being a hire car they're driving?

You've just found out the mysterious couple's names from the tags on their bags – *Dave Conn* and *Kate Dupe* – when you suddenly have an awful thought. Are they photo-journalists as well, but from a rival newspaper? A totally unscrupulous rival newspaper? Did they perhaps spot you on the plane and decide to take action to sabotage your assignment?

Your fears prove to be justified when the couple drop you off near the north-east corner of the mist-shrouded loch. As their car quickly disappears out of sight, you notice that your camera bag is suspiciously light. Hurriedly unzipping it, you discover that all your cameras and spare film have been removed and replaced by a rolled-up car rug!

You're in despair. The only camera that hasn't been stolen is your telephoto Polaroid. You'd kept this round your neck while you were in their car. But the film inside only has six exposures left. It's absolutely vital, therefore, that you don't waste a single shot . . .

Are you willing to undertake this difficult assignment? If so, turn the page . . .

◇ GAME INSTRUCTIONS ◇

1. For each attempt at the game, you must use one of the 40 score cards on the inside of the book's fold-out flaps. So your score card is as handy as possible during the game, always keep the appropriate flap *opened out* as you read through the book. (Right-handed readers will find it more convenient to use the score cards at the back of the book first, and left-handed readers those at the front.)

2. The 📷 column on your score card is for showing *the number of photographs you have left*, the 👹 column *the number of times you have snapped the monster on a photograph* and the 📇 column which *accessories* you have collected during the game.

📷 Column

3. At the start of the game you have **6** photographs in your Polaroid camera. Every time you take a photograph (either intentionally or by accident) during the game, you must reduce this score by one. You do this by using a pen or pencil to delete the top number showing in the 📷 column. So, for your first photograph taken you delete the **6**, for the second photograph the 5, the third the **4** . . . and so on.

4. When you have deleted every number down to and including **1**, it means that your film has run out and so you cannot continue with your assignment. If

◇ GAME INSTRUCTIONS ◇

you wish to make another attempt at the game, you must start all over again from the beginning (using a fresh score card).

📷 Column

5. If one of the photographs you take shows the monster, then you must also mark the 📷 column on your score card. For your first monster photograph circle the **1** in that column, for the second circle the **2** and so on.
6. Most of the photographs you take won't show the monster at all. You might *think* that you have snapped the monster, but when you turn to the paragraph that shows how the photo develops a few seconds later, the result will often prove disappointing. The developed photo might just show a seal or otter in the loch, someone in a distant rowing-boat . . . or simply a floating log.
7. The more times you attempt the game, though, the more skilful you'll become at working out whether to use your camera or not. So your 📷 score should become better and better.
8. Your ultimate aim is to take the maximum of **6** photographs showing the monster. Only **6** clear Loch Ness monster photographs will provide absolute confirmation that it exists . . . and give both you and your newspaper a brilliant reputation!

◇ GAME INSTRUCTIONS ◇

📖 Column

9. There are three useful *accessories* to be picked up during the game: a map, a local newspaper and a nature trail guide. These are depicted on the outside of the book's fold-out flaps. Possession of these accessories will greatly improve your chances of succeeding at the assignment and so you should make every effort to find them during the game.

10. If you *do* pick up one of the accessories, show this on your score card by using your pen or pencil to circle that accessory's code letter (M = MAP, N = NEWSPAPER and G = nature trail GUIDE) in the 📖 column. This means that you are then entitled to *consult* this particular accessory where appropriate during the game. On such occasions, simply select the flap showing that accessory and tuck it in *next* to the page you're reading.

11. Any accessory not circled on your score card may NOT be folded over and consulted at any point during the game.

1

You feel as if you're in the middle of nowhere. This narrow road where that odious Dave Conn and Kate Dupe dropped you off couldn't be more desolate. You haven't seen one other vehicle here yet! But as you start to follow the lonely road southwards, you discover that it at least provides you with excellent views of the loch. In fact, the road seems to hug the shore all the way. True, there are often trees screening the water but where there are clearings you can see right across the misty loch to the other side. The next clearing you reach is a particularly good one and you wonder whether you should start your first watch for the monster here. Or maybe there will be an even better viewing place a little further along the road. Your map of the loch would have told you, of course, but this too was in your camera bag . . . and this too was pinched by those tricksters!

What will you do?
  If stop here   go to 162
  If continue   go to 58

2

Having turned your camera to the left, you quickly focus it on the water. You desperately try to keep your hand from trembling with excitement as you wait. Suddenly, you can see a slight disturbance in the water through your view-finder: a few bubbles and strange ripples. Then something like a black snout starts to break the surface. Is this just one of the seals that inhabit the loch – or is it the monster itself? The 'snout' suddenly comes right out and you have just a split-second to decide whether to snap it or not!

If yes   go to 48
If no   go to 79

3

You've walked only a few metres on from the hotel when it suddenly occurs to you that you must be nearly halfway down the loch by now. Perhaps even further than that. There's no point walking too far south, of course, because all the sightings were reported at the northern end of the loch. You would do better to start searching for someone who might ferry you across so you can begin working your way up the other side. So, have you covered half the loch's length yet or not? What you really need to do is to look for that hotel on a local map . . .

If you have circled the MAP accessory you may consult it now to find out in which square the white hotel is situated. If you have not, you'll have to guess:
   If you think B4 go to 107
   If you think C4 go to 154
   If you think C3 go to 62

4

'I saw it about two hundred metres out there!' the woman tells you excitedly after you have followed her across the road. You decide to focus your camera on that part of the loch . . . but where is your camera? You suddenly remember that you'd momentarily put it down whilst in the phone box. Hurrying back there, you're horrified to see that Dave Conn is just about to slip inside. But he makes a run for it when he sees you coming, just before he can quite take your camera. His hand does just manage to reach the shutter release though so he can spitefully waste one of your precious photographs. Maggie Gordon has also now completely vanished. Except it wasn't Maggie Gordon at all, of course. It was obviously just Kate Dupe, diverting your attention!

Delete the top number in your score card's 📷 column. Go next to 136.

5

Unfortunately, your *first* guess was right! There was no monster there at all. ***Delete the top number in your score card's 📷 column. Go next to 142.***

6

As you're making your way down to the village's little bay, you start to wonder where this waterfall *is* exactly on the other side. You hope it's not anywhere *south* of where you are now, because you've already come far enough south as it is. It's something that you should perhaps check straightaway . . .

If you have circled the MAP accessory, you may study it now to find out which square the waterfall is in. If you haven't you'll have to guess:
  If you think B3   go to 29
  If you think C3   go to 120
  If you think B4   go to 71

7

Sitting down at this highest part of the bank, you start scanning the loch through your camera. Its powerful telephoto lens allows you to pick out even the smallest detail on the water – every single wave crest, even the occasional seagull alighting there. But for the moment that's all you can see. There's certainly no huge long neck sticking out! ***Go to 10.***

8

As you follow these 🐦 symbols, more and more light appears through the trees. You've soon risen right above the tree line and, as you'd hoped, you can see virtually from one end of the loch to the other. The water lies quiet and mysterious below you. Entranced, you watch it a while, hoping for some unusual waves moving down the loch. But, except for those small regular crests caused by the wind, the surface of the water remains undisturbed. Eventually, therefore, you make your way back down the mountain again towards the road. ***Go to 37.***

9

Having retraced part of the way down the footpath, you once more patiently watch that area of loch just behind the castle. The half-hour you permitted yourself is coming to an end when you suddenly notice something pole-like over on the far side of the water. Could it possibly be the monster's neck? You're just bringing your camera up to your eye so you can examine the object through your telephoto lens when it starts to move. You suddenly have no time for careful study . . . you must make a decision about taking a photograph right now!

Will you decide to take one or not?
   If yes   *go to 26*
   If no   *go to 49*

10

While you're waiting for something more interesting to appear on the loch, you wonder exactly how far down it you are. You remember driving past a small white inn on the road, about a mile before that despicable couple dropped you off. Since buildings are so rare around here, that inn would surely be shown on any map of the area. . .

But have you circled the MAP accessory? If you have, you may study it now to find out in which square the small white inn is situated. If you haven't, you'll have to guess:
   If you think E2   *go to 36*
   If you think D1   *go to 131*
   If you think D2   *go to 75*

11

'Well, are you staying or not?' the bus driver asks as you look back towards the door. 'If it's a photograph of the monster you're hoping for, you'd do better to wait until we're a little further up the loch anyway. That's where some folk say the monster can be seen: at one of three parking places at the side of this road. I'll tell you what, since there's no one else on the bus and we're not running late, I'll stop briefly at one of these three parking places if you like. Just tell me which you'd prefer: the first, second or third.'

Which will you choose?
If first   *go to 97*
If second *go to 113*
If third   *go to 56*

12

As you approach the jagged ruins of the tower, you wonder how far up the loch this castle is. Are you six miles from the top end here – or is it nearer eight? Or should you be even less optimistic than that and expect as many as twelve miles? Looking for the castle on a *map* of the loch would tell you, of course . . .

If you have circled the MAP accessory you may study it now to find out which square the castle is in. If you haven't, you'll have to guess:
  If you think C2   go to 108
  If you think C3   go to 43
  If you think B3   go to 157

13

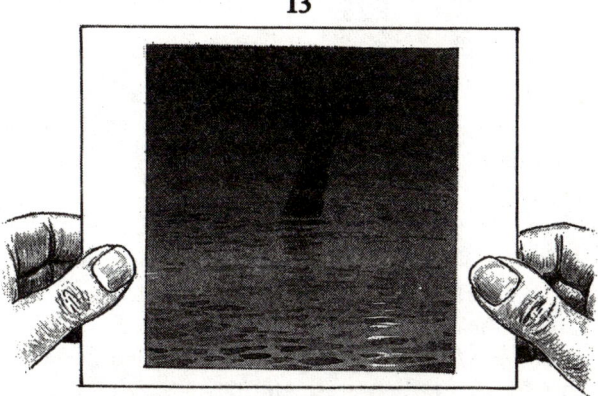

Well done – the monster's head and neck are just about visible! Record this success in the 📷 *column of your score card. Also, delete the top number in the* 📷 *column to show that you have used another photograph. Now go to 65.*

14

You almost stop panting as you follow the trail marked by the 🐿 symbols. This is because the ascent is much more gentle now, the trail twisting and turning rather than taking a more direct route. But the trail *does* take a more direct route on the way down again, soon returning you to the road. This you're grateful for . . . because you saw absolutely no evidence of the monster whatsoever from up there! ***Go to 37.***

15

You decide to follow the road to the left because you're sure you heard the car speed off to the *right*. But you've gone only a few steps in this direction when the doubts start to set in. You were still trying to disentangle yourself from that blanket after all, when the car sped off. It might have confused you. But then you catch sight of a signpost further along the road. With any luck, you say to yourself, it should give the mileage to the loch. But it doesn't, unfortunately. It points only to a Stone Age burial mound. You need to look for that mound on a map . . .

If you have circled the MAP accessory you may consult it now to find out in which square the burial mound (a heap of rocks with an entrance at the bottom) is. If you haven't, you'll have to guess:
  If you think B1 go to 112
  If you think B2 go to 77
  If you think A2 go to 91

16
Unfortunately, the next passing place *does* prove to be quite some distance away, and you still haven't reached it. But you've walked far too far now to go all the way back again. Visibility down to barely two metres in front of you, you only hope that the virtual non-existence of cars along this road continues! Mercifully, you at last arrive at the next passing place. And, as luck would have it, the moment you do, the rain decides to stop! ***Go to 54.***

17

You eagerly scan the water here to see if anything unusual starts to disturb its surface. You remember that home movie showing a strange wake on the water. A wake travelling much faster, apparently, than one which would be caused by a simple rowing-boat! It looks like your hopes for a repeat performance are in vain, though. But what's that right over in the distance? A V-shaped wave that is far too long to have been caused by the wind suddenly appears there, moving at quite a speed! You hurriedly direct your camera to the surf at the front of the wave before it passes out of range. Do you snap a photo of this or not?

If yes   go to 55
If no   go to 142

18

'Hello, are you looking for my husband, the minister?' a friendly woman asks after you have knocked at the house. 'He's in the church at the moment. Feel free to wander across there and go inside.' You ask if *she* might be able to help you, though, to save you time. 'Oh, I believe I can,' she replies when you've told her about your need of a boat. 'Just go down to the village's wee bay and seek out a Davie MacGregor. There's no mistaking him because he always wears a bright orange woolly hat!' ***Go to 57.***

19

Your eyes are straining so hard at the loch, desperate to make the most of this last chance, that they start to ache. So you move them away from the water for a brief while, focusing on something else. You choose the bus timetable just in front of you. The next stop along the loch, you read, is at the Wellington bomber memorial. Yes, didn't a Wellington bomber crash in the loch during the War? You wonder if this memorial is significant enough to be shown on a map of the loch...

If you have circled the MAP accessory you may study it now to find out which square the memorial is in. If you haven't, you'll have to guess:
   If you think D1   go to 159
   If you think C1   go to 94
   If you think E1   go to 80

20

The fallen tree is still little more than a speck across the water when you notice something directly in line with it. Bobbing up and down in the choppy loch is a strange angular shape. 'Oh, that will just be another fallen tree,' your oarsman tells you, glancing over his shoulder. 'One that's rolled right down into the water.' You're not sure you agree with him, however. If only he would take a better look! But it's too late – the shape has disappeared. No, it hasn't. It's suddenly bobbed up again. If you're going to take a photo you'd better do so right now in case it disappears *completely* next time . . .

If decide on a photo   **go to 63**
If decide against it   **go to 141**

21

Certain that this is Dave Conn, you immediately start clambering back up the bank again. 'What's wrong?' the bewildered monk calls after you. You ignore him, though, continuing your hurried scramble up towards the road. Suddenly, you lose your footing. The next thing you know you're tumbling back down the slope towards the water! Fortunately, the monk just manages to intercept your path and save you. Much to your embarrassment, you realise that he obviously *is* genuine after all. And, as you later say goodbye to him, you have a second awful realisation. You'd accidentally hit the shutter button on your camera during that tumble. You have used up a precious photograph!

Delete the top number in your score card's 📷 column. Go next to 37.

22

It's just an upturned rowing-boat which must have broken loose from its moorings in the storm! ***Delete the top number in your score card's 📷 column. Go next to 51.***

23

As you'd already noticed from the other side, the slopes are even steeper on this western side of the loch. And darker too; dense with fir-trees! You pass a rough track climbing up between these firs. It's only when this track is some distance behind you that you rather regret not taking it. You'd probably have had extensive views of the loch as the track climbed. And, who knows, maybe a long-distance view of the monster as well! So you wonder whether you should turn round and make your way back there . . . or, at least, resolve to take the very next forest track that you pass. Or perhaps it's more sensible just to keep following this shore road.

What will you decide?
If return to last track   go to 134
If continue to next   go to 147
If keep to shore road   go to 163

24

You now hurriedly make your way back up the steep rocky slope to the bus stop. If it's on time, the bus should be coming along very soon. As you clamber up over the rocks, though, you notice a faded postcard lying amongst them. The photograph on it shows a stone drinking well, built over a small brook in the trees. Since the last time you had a drink was a good nine hours ago, you wonder if this quaint little well is nearby.

If you have circled the MAP accessory you may study it now to find out which square the drinking well is in. If you haven't, you'll have to guess:
　If you think B2　go to 78
　If you think B1　go to 116
　If you think A1　go to 148

25

Peering out towards the south end of the loch, you only hope that if the monster is to appear in that direction, it appears no more than a few dozen metres away from you. That's about as far as you can see through these lashing sweeps of rain! Suddenly, though, something *does* show itself very vaguely in the distance. You can just see something dark and rounded bobbing amongst the turbulent waves. Could it be the monster's head? It's moving fast beyond your limited range of vision, though, and so if a photo is to be taken at all, it must be done right now!

If you wish to take photo   go to 70
If you don't   go to 51

26

Well snapped! Record this success in the 📷 column of your score card. Also, delete the top number in your score card's 📷 column to show that you have used another photo. Go next to 49.

27

This branch of the footpath rapidly becomes steeper and you're soon panting for breath. But it means that a good open view of the loch appears fairly quickly and so you now have your question answered – you need to follow that road to the right for about four miles. Because the trail is equally steep in its descent, it's not too long before you're returning to the road: exhausted but at least now knowing in which direction to head!
Go to 149.

28

Having climbed down the rough steps of the bank, you find yourself standing on a narrow strip of beach covered with large pebbles. The loch's gentle waves break only metres in front of you. You again squint right across the eerie strip of water to the other side, and you can just make out a hotel there, set back from the shore. You wonder if the brightly coloured flags in front of it mean that it's a yachting hotel. A map would be sure to tell you. . .

But have you circled the MAP accessory? If you have, you may study it now to find out in which square the hotel with the flags is situated. If not, you'll have to guess:
  If you think B2   go to 98
  If you think C2   go to 75
  If you think C3   go to 121

29

Anxious that you might miss Davie MacGregor and his boat if you dally here too long, you immediately continue making your way down to the village's little bay. You know that he will be heading for the opposite shore, even if it's not exactly the part you want. It's not an opportunity you can afford to waste! *Go to 57.*

30

As you're staring straight ahead, a mist starts to drift across the water. It becomes thicker and thicker, soon with only a few 'gaps' here and there. What terrible luck! Suddenly, though, the monster's head and neck rear up in one of these gaps. You quickly prepare your camera to take a photograph. The gap is now rapidly getting smaller, though; the mists enveloping the monster. Will a photograph be worth it?

If decide yes go to 84
If decide no   go to 68

31

Continuing your long walk back to the loch, you eventually reach a small stone church. At last – something that's likely to be marked on the map, telling you exactly where you are! But do you possess a map?

If you have circled the MAP accessory you may study it now to find out which square the church is in. If you haven't, you'll have to guess:
   If you think B2   go to 149
   If you think B3   go to 115
   If you think A2   go to 73

32

'Here, what are you doing? Ye'll have us both in the water!' the man exclaims as you suddenly try to snatch the oars from him. But you're sure that's exactly what he was planning – or at least, he was planning to tip just *you* into the water. When he has finally managed to seize the oars back from you, however, he merely rows you quickly and safely back to shore. He drops you off before angrily rowing away. So he *was* Jamie MacTavish after all. And not only did you make a fool of yourself when you made a grab for his oars . . . you now discover that you accidentally took a photograph as well.

Delete the top number in your score card's 📷 column. Go next to 24.

33

Bad luck! Delete the top number in your score card's 📷 column. Go next to 68.

34

'Excuse me!' you call out to the tractor driver as you let the cyclist pass. By the time the farmer has steered his awkward vehicle towards you and switched off its engine, the walker has passed you both as well. 'Now let me guess,' the farmer says with a chuckle, noticing the camera dangling from your neck, 'it's that wee monster ye'll be interested in? I must confess, I've ne'er seen it myself but I know many folk that have. There have been sightings all the way along this road. One spot's just as likely as the next. Just keep your eyes peeled and maybe it'll be your lucky day!' ***Go to 146.***

35

Twice you nearly slip on the treacherous road, but you're soon approaching that last passing place. You can just make out a small post van at the far end. Presumably, the postman has stopped there to stretch his legs for a moment. You decide to go and talk to him. But before you reach the van it does a neat three-point turn and then quickly disappears in the other direction! You do have one piece of good fortune, though. In fact, two . . . ***Go to 139.***

36

You can't help feeling annoyed that you're unable to find out where the inn is. You're annoyed with that couple of tricksters – and annoyed with yourself. If only you had kept your map in your anorak pocket instead of your camera bag! As for Dave Conn and Kate Dupe – wouldn't you just like to lay your hands on them! Your fingers instinctively tighten round your camera at this vengeful thought. So tightly though, that you now have another reason for despising them both. You've accidentally pressed your camera's shutter release and wasted a precious photograph!

Delete the top number in your score card's 📷 column. Go next to 75.

37

You have gone only a short way further along this western shore road when a second storm suddenly whips up over the loch. This one's even fiercer, drawing a dark sinister veil over the water. Fortunately, you notice a deserted hut on the loch side of the road, a little way down the bank, and so you hurry there for shelter. Crouching inside, you see that it has a shuttered open window at the front and you guess that this was once a monster-watcher's hut! You decide that you might as well use it for this purpose yourself. But you can't make up your mind whether you should look towards the north end of the loch, the south or straight ahead . . .

Which will you eventually decide?
  If towards north end   *go to 69*
  If towards south end   *go to 25*
  If straight ahead   *go to 126*

38

Looking around the cramped, dilapidated hut, you realise that your scramble down here *was* a waste of time after all. The hut obviously hasn't been used for years and years. Far from there being any fascinating notes still lying around, there's nothing inside but two badly-rotted chairs. You're just ducking your head so you can step outside again, when you slip on one of the slimy floorboards. Now you have a second reason for being annoyed that you chose to come down here. You knocked your camera's shutter release as you slipped and wasted a photograph!

Delete the top number in your score card's 📷 column. Go next to 119.

39

Reaching the village's small church, you're disappointed to see that there's no one about. You'd hoped you might spot the minister there, or his wife, or a gardener raking up the fallen leaves. Perhaps one of these will be found at the back of the church, though. You're just about to make your way round there when you wonder if you'd have more luck actually going inside the church. Or maybe you should knock at the house next door. It looks as if this might be where the minister lives. . .

Which will you choose?
   If go behind church   *go to 66*
   If enter church   *go to 102*
   If knock at house   *go to 18*

40

You haven't left the telephone box far behind when a black Labrador comes running up to you. You keep trying to shoo it away but it's determined that you should be friends! 'Don't worry, she won't bite,' you hear a voice call out as a man appears behind you as well. Turning round, you see that he wears exactly the same type of oilskin jacket – dark green with a brown corduroy collar – as one of those witnesses in that news item about the monster! ***Go to 117.***

41

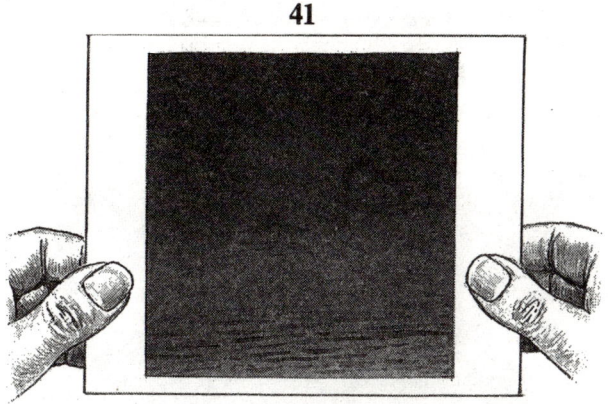

Unfortunately the monster isn't sufficiently distinct from the darkness. So you can't use this photo as proof. ***Delete the top number in your score card's 📷 column. Go next to 65.***

42

'What's that large dark thing just below the surface of the water?' you suddenly ask after Davie has rowed you some way nearer the boulders. You quickly focus your camera on the spot while Davie sceptically glances over his shoulder. His scepticism immediately disappears, though, as the monster's huge neck suddenly rises up from the water! He drops his oars in shock, the boat starting to rock as the waves turn it off its path. If you take a photo now, there's a high risk it will be blurred. But if you don't, the monster might suddenly submerge, not to reappear! What should you do?

If take photo   *go to 133*
If decide not to   *go to 141*

43

Reaching the top of the crumbling tower, you nervously look down on the sinister black water some twenty metres below. You remember reading that the loch is at its very deepest here! You're just imagining what at this very moment might be moving around in those eerie depths when you hear someone shout up at you from the grassland behind the tower. It's a man in a peaked cap and you assume he's a farmer. ***Go to 125.***

44

No monster . . . but there's a huge whirlpool effect only about fifty metres straight in front of you! The monster must have surfaced and immediately dived under again. You eagerly raise your camera to your eyes, praying that it will repeat this. But where do you point your camera? The same spot . . . or would the monster be more likely to re-emerge much further to the left or right of this?

Where will you direct your camera?
 If to left   go to 2
 If straight ahead   go to 135
 If to right   go to 60

45

As you start waiting those forty-five minutes at the bus stop, you realise that this is your very last opportunity to photograph the monster. By the time the bus comes the light will surely have completely faded. Even if it hasn't quite gone, it wouldn't be sensible for you suddenly to disembark from the bus at some point. The timetable shows that the bus after that, the very last service of the day, is not for another three hours! ***Go to 53.***

46

Although you step right to the very edge of the castle's tower, as the farmer had instructed, you still can't see anything below. 'Surely you must be able to by now?' he yells up frantically. 'Well, try leaning over a bit further then. Don't worry, it's perfectly safe.' Again, you do as the farmer instructs . . . but then you suddenly feel the stone wall crumble away under your feet. You leap back only just in time! Furious, you turn back towards the farmer – but he's suddenly disappeared. So it obviously *was* Dave Conn after all. But that's not your only infuriating discovery. You find that you accidentally pressed the camera's shutter release and took a photograph when you leapt back from the tower's edge!

Delete the top number in your score card's 📷 column. Go next to 105.

47

Well, this choice of trail certainly is steep in its ascent, you say to yourself between pants. Unfortunately, though, the route it takes down is much gentler and therefore slower. You don't return to the road until a good thirty minutes after you'd left it. But at least following that trail gave you the information you needed. The loch was clearly visible from the top – and it lies to the west of where you are now. In other words, you must walk to the *right* along this road. ***Go to 149.***

48

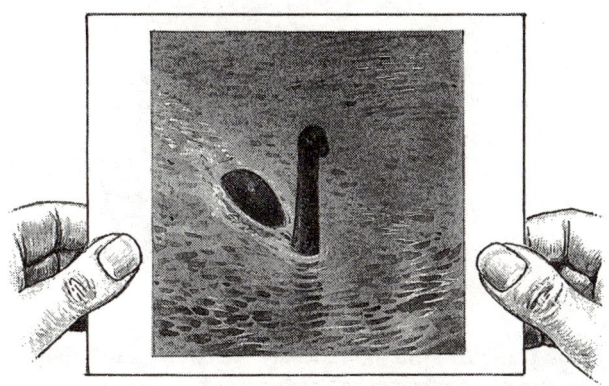

Well snapped! Your first photo of the monster! Record this in the 📷 column of your score card. Also, delete the top number in the 📷 column. Go next to 79.

49

This time you really do make your departure from the castle, resuming your trek along the road. You've gone only a mile or so further when you reach the little village of Drumnadrochit. There's a tiny bus stop in the village and you study the timetable there to see how frequent the buses are along this road. *You* certainly haven't encountered one yet! You're still trying to make sense of the timetable when suddenly everything goes dark. A blanket has been thrown over your head! And now you're being quickly and roughly pushed into a car . . . ***Go to 110.***

50

This trail turns out to be a really *bad* choice. Although it provides many views, it's very long, taking you further and further from the bus stop. You decide you can't risk the circular walk – it might take hours for all you know – and so you immediately start to retrace your steps. You're in such a hurry that, just before you rejoin that footpath back to the road, you trip on a fallen branch. You hear a depressing click from your camera as you hit the ground.

Delete the top number in your score card's 📷 column. Go next to 148.

51

At last the fierce sweeps of rain become no more than a drizzle. So you now leave the observation hut and continue your long walk northwards. You've clocked up another mile or so when you spot the loch's most famous landmark just below you. It's a ruined castle standing on a grassy mound jutting out into the loch. Recalling that many of the most famous monster sightings have been from this castle, you make your way down there. You wonder which part of the castle to head for: the ruined tower at one end or its crumbling walls at the other.

Which will you decide on?
  If tower   go to 12
  If walls   go to 155

52

As you stare to the left across the loch, disaster strikes. A mist rapidly appears, thick drifts of it masking the water. You're just going to have to wait until it lifts . . . as if time wasn't critical enough anyway! But at least large holes open up in the mist every so often and it is through one of these holes that you suddenly think you can see two dark humps. The hole is closing up again, however, and so there's no time to study the humps properly before taking a photograph. If you *are* going to take one, it must be right now!

If take photo   go to 140
If not   go to 68

53

You're soon becoming rather more optimistic about your chances of spotting the monster before you have to board the bus. For you notice that the mist over the loch is rapidly lifting. At this rate, visibility should be almost perfect again in a few minutes. So you start to wonder if you would do better to climb up the slope behind the bus stop for a wider view. Or maybe climb down from it so you can be right at the water's edge. But what if the bus is a little early, though, and you miss it? Perhaps it would be best, therefore, to remain right where you are.

What will you decide to do?
If climb above stop   *go to 128*
If climb down from stop *go to 153*
If remain at stop   *go to 19*

54
You've continued quite a way further down the eastern side of the loch when you come upon a phone box at the side of the road. There is nothing else here, and you wonder who on earth would have cause to use it in such

a desolate place! But YOU are certainly grateful that it's there. It means that you can ring your editor and let him know of your misfortune of losing so much of your equipment. But then you wonder whether this would be an unnecessary waste of time. After all, what's happened has happened, and so perhaps you should just continue on your way. What will you decide?

If enter phone box   go to 114
If continue past it   go to 40

55

Unfortunately, it was just a speeding motor-boat. ***Delete the top number in your score card's 📷 column. Go next to 142.***

56

After the bus has passed the first two parking places, you wonder if you were mad to have chosen the third. Surely that last trace of light will have completely gone by the time you reach it. The place is only another half mile away, however, and your hopes are resurrected by the fact that the moon has now appeared over the loch. And, indeed, the monster's dark silhouette does suddenly appear in that twinkling pool of silver! But only a moment later a large wispy cloud passes over the moon. You're sure the monster's shape is still just about visible . . . but will it be so on the photograph?

If take photo   *go to 41*
If not   *go to 65*

57

It looks as if you're too late because, when you arrive down at the bay, you spot Davie MacGregor in his orange hat already rowing his little boat out into the loch. Fortunately, though, he responds to your frantic waving and, curious, he rows back to within earshot of your shouts. 'Ay, I'd be happy enough to take you to the other side of the loch,' he shouts across the water. 'Your fare will be just the price of a wee whisky. Have we a deal?' Yes, you most certainly have – and you're soon in his little rowing-boat, bobbing up and down with him on the dark, rather eerie loch. ***Go to 138.***

58

You have walked only a little way beyond the clearing when you at last spot someone else. It's another walker, coming the other way. You decide to stop him so you can ask how far it is to the best viewing places that he would have passed. But then a touring cyclist appears round the corner behind him. Perhaps *he* would be a better person to ask. Then a slow-moving tractor suddenly appears as well. The driver would live locally, of course. So perhaps it's *him* you should have a chat with . . .

Whom will you eventually decide on?
   If walker   *go to 82*
   If cyclist   *go to 130*
   If tractor driver *go to 34*

59

'I'm worried we'll miss the bus if we wander too far from the stop,' you say, making your excuse as you suddenly halt behind the woman. 'I'm sure we won't,' she insists, reaching out for your arm. But as she does so, her black hair begins to slide from her head! It's just a wig. There's the blonde Kate Dupe underneath! But a Kate Dupe who is now fast hurrying away into the darkness . . . ***Go to 148***.

60

As you point your camera over to the right, you feel certain that you're making the correct decision. It's a good half minute now since you heard that splash and the monster would surely have travelled a fair distance in that time. You've just focused your camera on an area of the water when some strange-looking ripples appear through the view-finder. You think you can make out something moving just below the surface! Suddenly, a dark shape emerges and you have immediately to decide whether to snap it or not in case it straightaway dives down again. . .

If yes   go to 100
If no   go to 79

61

Well, at least there's no real chance of your slipping at this slow pace. You would hate to drop your camera – or end up sprawled in the middle of the road! But now you're greatly increasing the risk of encountering a vehicle at some point. So you feel constantly tense as you trudge on through the blinding rain. It stings your face and you wonder how much further you can go. Where on earth *was* that passing place? As it turns out, the rain suddenly stops before you reach the place so you just have to turn right round again and make your way back to where you were before! ***Go to 54.***

62

You're only a short distance further from the hotel when you hear a huge splash coming from the loch. You hurriedly make your way through the trees, camera at the ready. You're in a bit too much of a hurry, though, because you trip on the tangled undergrowth. . . hitting your camera's shutter release as you fall! And there's more disappointment for you. When you finally reach the edge of the water, you see a large log floating there. So *that* was the cause of the splash. Someone must have just thrown it in – and you can guess *who*. You'd bet every penny you have that those two devious journalists are hiding somewhere nearby!

Delete the top number in your score card's 📷 column. Go next to 107.

You should have taken Davie's word for it! ***Delete the top number in your score card's 📷 column. Go next to 141.***

64

Just as you thought . . . this is Dave Conn planning something nasty for you. For he suddenly reaches down and picks up a heavy stick! It's a good job you were prepared for this. You quickly turn on your heels and run before he has time to swing round and hit you over the head. But as you continue hurrying back towards the road, you see that he doesn't swing round at all. And the stick is merely to throw for his dog! So it *is* Angus MacDonald after all, you realise. In your confusion, though, you trip over a branch and fall heavily to the ground. Not only are you too embarrassed by your actions to return to Angus now – but you see that you accidentally took a photo as well!

Delete the top number in your score card's 📷 column. Go next to 136.

65

Re-boarding the bus, you accept that your opportunities for photographing the monster are at last definitely over. Your single concern now is that you get back to Inverness Airport in time for your plane! You find yourself a genuine taxi this time, though, and so you just make it. You're equally lucky at the other end. Only ten minutes after the plane has touched down, a taxi is speeding you back to your newspaper's offices. You should just beat the deadline for tomorrow morning's issue! But will the photographs you've brought back from Loch Ness make that issue a world sensation. . . ?

Remember: just one photograph of the Loch Ness monster will cause a huge stir . . . two or three even more so. To provide absolute proof that the monster exists, however, you need to have taken the whole six photographs. So, if your final total wasn't six, try the game again to see if you can improve on your score.

66

You're in luck! Wandering round to the back of the church, you *do* find a gardener tidying up the leaves. Leaning on his rake, he recommends that you go and search out a man called Davie MacGregor who has a rowing-boat moored at the village's little bay. And who is unmistakable because of his bright orange woolly hat! 'Exploring round the loch, are ye?' the gardener asks. 'Perhaps this nature trail guide would come in handy, then? It must have blown in from the road. I was going to chuck it in the rubbish bag with the leaves but you're welcome to it if you like!'

You are now entitled to use the GUIDE on the back flap of this book. Circle the G in the 📖 column of your score card so that you have a reminder of this whenever the guide is required. Go next to 57.

67

Following the ✦ symbols, you find that this trail does occasionally offer a view of the loch below. But it's never a very extensive view because there's still a fair density of trees along most of the route. The trail finally brings you steeply down back towards the road but, just before you reach it, you slip on some of the damp undergrowth. You wince on hearing a loud click from your camera. That's a precious photograph wasted!

Delete the top number in your score card's 📷 column. Go next to 37.

68

The mist has now obscured the loch completely and so you decide you might just as well continue your walk towards its top end. You'll just have to hope visibility clears at least once more before darkness sets in. But that's surely less than an hour away now! You've walked about a mile further when you come across another bus stop. It seems far too remote a place for anyone to want to catch a bus – but there's certainly *one* person who can make use of it. Yourself! And you see that there's a bus due in just three quarters of an hour. And it goes all the way back to Inverness! ***Go to 45.***

69

You haven't been looking towards the north end of the loch for long when a dark hump suddenly appears in the turbulent water. At least, you *think* it's a hump. It's so difficult to tell through this lashing storm. It's all just a grey blur out there! The dark shape becomes slightly clearer, though, and you're now fairly confident it *is* a hump. You must quickly decide whether to catch it on film or not before it's obscured by another sweep of rain . . .

If take photo   *go to 22*
If decide not to   *go to 51*

70

It's a stray marker buoy in the water! **Delete the top number in your score card's 📷 column. Go 51.**

71

Since you don't have a map with you, you hurry back to the grocer to check where this waterfall is exactly on the other side. 'Oh, it's about two miles north of here,' he says. 'A magnificent waterfall it is –' But you're already out of his shop again, making your way back to the little bay. If the waterfall is *two miles to the north* and this Davie MacGregor moors his boat about *two miles south of it*, then he must row almost straight across the loch. Why couldn't the grocer have just told you that in the first place! ***Go to 57.***

72

'I'm afraid I haven't got time,' you tell the woman politely but firmly. She's not to be deterred, though. Her arm reaches for yours anyway – or rather for your camera! Fortunately, you are enough on your guard to stop her. As you're doing so, however, your camera slips off your neck and falls to the ground. 'I was only trying to *catch* your camera for you,' the woman says with a huff as she walks off. 'I could see that the knot on the neck strap was working itself loose!' What a shame you hadn't trusted the woman . . . for your camera, although not damaged fortunately, had taken a photograph as it hit the ground!

Delete the top number in your score card's 📷 column. Go next to 105.

73

Since you don't have a map, you try to think how else you can estimate the distance back to the loch. Now, how long were you in that car? No more than ten minutes, surely? So it might be only three or four miles. But they *were* driving very fast. Perhaps it's nearer eight or nine, then! You can only hope that, because you were under a blanket, the car's speed seemed much faster to you than it actually was . . . ***Go to 149.***

74

You make your way back down to the castle and stand right underneath it once more, at the very edge of the loch. Suddenly, you notice something way over to your right. There's a small bend in the shoreline there – and out from behind that bend slowly drifts what looks like a greyish hump. Could this be the monster? You're just about to focus your camera on this hump when, to your astonishment, it suddenly reverses. You're becoming rather suspicious about it, but there's no time to pursue this suspicion. The hump is about to disappear again behind the bend. So do you quickly take a photograph or not?

If yes   go to 118
If no   go to 49

75

You continue your watch at this clearing for another twenty minutes or so but it's completely without success. You haven't spotted so much as an unusual

ripple on the water yet, let alone something actually rising up from it! So you decide to make your way a little further down the road. You've just turned your back on the clearing, however, when you hear an almighty splash right behind you. Holding your breath, you swing round, expecting to see the monster there . . .
Go to 44.

76

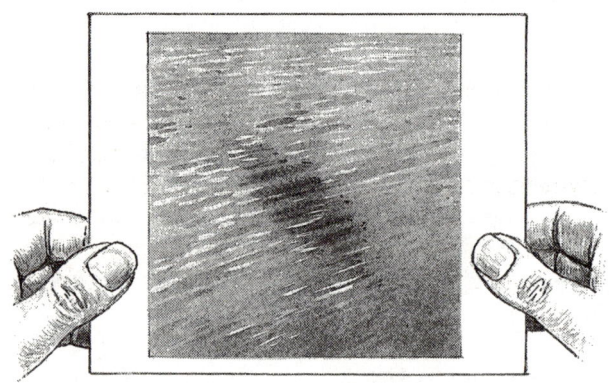

Unfortunately you were just too late. The monster's hump has completely submerged again and this dark shape under the water could be anything. Your photo will not stand up as proof of the monster's existence. ***Delete the top number in your score card's 📷 column. Go next to 49.***

77

Once again, you become annoyed with yourself for letting that odious couple pinch your map during that 'taxi ride' from the airport. Suddenly, there they are again, though – the car comes screeching round a corner ahead. They gloat at you from behind the windscreen as they speed past. You try not to let this anger you, however. At least you now know to walk in the *other* direction for the loch. For they're obviously returning that way themselves . . . ***Go to 149.***

78

Since you don't have a map with you, you'll never know whether that little drinking well is nearby or not. You could have really done with it. You haven't had anything to drink since a morning cup of coffee on the plane. Nor to eat, come to that. You did bring refreshments with you but they were in the side pocket of your camera bag. The camera bag that was stealthily emptied, of course, by that vile couple! ***Go to 148.***

79

Since you observe no further disturbances on the water from here, this time you really do make your departure from the clearing. You've walked quite a way further along the narrow road when it starts to rain. You raise your anorak hood, hoping that the rain won't get any heavier. It does, though. It becomes fiercer and fiercer, pounding the road and blinding your eyes. It makes you increasingly anxious . . . ***Go to 143.***

80

Glancing at that timetable for a moment seems to have done the trick! For when you return your stare to the loch, everything seems a lot sharper. But it's not long before the water appears to blur in front of you again. For dusk is rapidly falling. It's becoming more and more difficult to work out what is water and what is sky. Let alone if there might be a dark shape in that water! ***Go to 159.***

81

'This is the place, right here!' Mrs Campbell exclaims after walking a few steps more. 'I was looking straight ahead, towards that white house on the other side. You can just about see it if you stand right at the edge of the bank here.' As you move towards the top of the steep slope, though, Mrs Campbell (or rather Kate Dupe!) suddenly gives you a hard push in the back and then runs off. Fortunately, you just manage to throw yourself backwards, away from the treacherous slope. But it costs you. For, as you fall, you jolt your camera, causing a photograph to be taken.

Delete the top number in your score card's 📷 column. Go next to 148.

82

'The best viewing places along the loch,' the walker considers, scratching his beard, after you have let both the cyclist and the tractor pass. 'Well, it all depends what exactly you want a view *of*,' he adds. 'Is it the mountains, the historical sites or just the loch itself?' You tell him that what you're really interested in is the monster. You expect him to be excited by this but his friendliness suddenly vanishes. 'Oh, I've got no time for that nonsense!' he retorts irritably. 'I assumed you were a *proper* nature lover like myself. Not some empty-headed tourist!' And with a gruff 'good day' he brushes past you. ***Go to 146.***

83

'I take it you're a newspaper photographer here to try and snap a photo of the monster?' the man asks, glancing down at your camera. 'I was one of those people who witnessed it. It was just over there, through the trees. Come, I'll show you!' As he steps towards you, however, he suddenly tries to grab your camera! Fortunately, you were prepared for this and manage to yank it out of his reach – but you knock the shutter release button in the process. You hear Jock Reid's malicious snigger as he runs off up the road. Or should you say Dave Conn's!

Delete the top number in your score card's 📷 column. Go next to 107.

84

Well risked! Record this success in the 🎞 column of your score card. Also, delete the top number in the 📷 column to show that you have used another photograph. Go next to 68.

85

'Well, are you coming to see where I spotted the monster or not?' the woman asks, trying to lead you out of the phone box. You shake your head, telling her that you haven't really got time. She starts to take offence. 'Well, you've got enough time to hog that phone all day,' she replies angrily. 'Perhaps there are others who would like to use it too!' So, to avoid trouble, you step out of the phone box and continue on your way. You'll just have to forget about ringing your editor. You weren't really looking forward to it anyway! ***Go to 136.***

86

This trail turns out to be the very *opposite* of what you were hoping for. The path has a steep climb and then a gentle descent! So you reach the top absolutely exhausted and your return down to the road along the loch takes much longer than you would have liked. What makes it worse is that you didn't see anything from the top anyway. True, there was a magnificent full view of the loch, but you didn't observe one strange wave on its surface, or one sudden whirlpool. All that effort was for nothing. What a waste of your precious time! ***Go to 37.***

87

'Ye'll be wanting someone to row ye across the loch, will ye?' the elderly postmistress asks when you have entered her shop. 'Now let me see. Let me see,' she considers, tapping her pen on the counter. 'Jock MacPhee will sometimes take a tourist over but he was out all last night fishing and so he's nae doubt sleeping the day off. Your best bet is probably Davie Mac-Gregor. I believe he and his boat are going to make a trip across this very afternoon. If ye hurry down to the village's wee bay ye might just catch him. You'll know him because he always wears a bright orange woolly hat!' ***Go to 57.***

88

This trail is just what you wanted. It does afford you *some* views of the slowly darkening loch but it brings you back to the bus stop with plenty of time still in hand. The only unfortunate part about your little detour is that those views didn't include a sighting of the monster! ***Go to 148***.

89

'Ah, you've missed it!' the farmer calls up contemptuously, shaking his head. 'Why didn't you go right to the edge of the tower like I told you? It's perfectly safe there. Don't you trust me?' He shakes his head a bit *too* much, though, because one of his bushy sideboards suddenly drops off. 'No, I most certainly don't, Mr Conn!' you shout mockingly after him as he scurries, red-faced, well away from there. ***Go to 105***.

90

Allowing the woman to take your arm, you then follow her to where the castle walls are at their highest. 'This is exactly where I was standing, right here!' she tells you excitedly as she makes you stop. Unfortunately, though, it doesn't look as if the monster is going to put in a second appearance here for you. You both wait and watch the loch for a good twenty minutes, but without success. 'Oh well, I suppose two days running *was* a bit much to hope for,' the woman says with a sigh and she bids you goodbye. ***Go to 105***.

91

A map isn't necessary after all, though, because a car suddenly appears on the road ahead. It comes screeching round the corner and blares its horn as it speeds past you, nearly knocking you over. It's that wretched couple again! They obviously turned round further up the road so they could make their way back to the loch.

So you now turn round yourself, knowing that you're definitely going in the *right* direction this time. The only question is . . . how many miles will it be? ***Go to 149.***

92

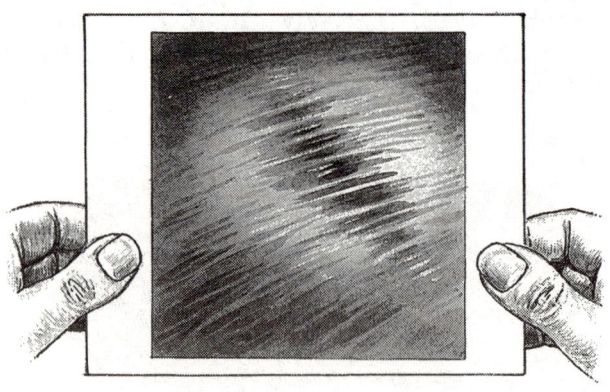

Unfortunately, it wasn't bright enough for a conclusive photograph. ***Delete the top number in your score card's 📷 column. Go next to 65.***

93

As you're staring to the right over the loch, you are horrified to see a thick mist suddenly sweep across the water. What chance is there of spotting something now? Suddenly, though, a hole begins to open up in the mist and you're sure you can see the faint silhouette of a hump and neck there. Or is it just a fisherman sitting at one end of his rowing-boat? You're about to look through your camera to work out *which* it is, when the hole starts to close quickly again. But there isn't time for careful examination. Any photographs must be taken straightaway!

If take photo   go to 33
If not   go to 68

94

The trick seems to have worked. For as you now return your eyes to the loch, everything seems much sharper. Dusk is falling so rapidly over the water, though, that it's not long before your eyes are starting to strain again. You try looking through your camera to see if the telephoto lens makes things any clearer. Only very slightly. Perhaps if you put your eye right against the view-finder . . . oh no! You've gripped the camera so tightly that you inadvertently pressed the shutter release button.

Delete the top number in your score card's 📷 column. Go next to 159.

95

Having rowed you some two hundred metres out into the loch, Jamie suddenly raises his oars from the deep, black water. He tells you to be absolutely quiet and still. After a good quarter of an hour has passed in this silent and tense watch, however, he takes up his oars and starts to row you back to the shore. 'Ye'll miss that bus of yours if we wait any longer,' he says with a sigh. 'It looks like that monster is not going to be quite as sociable today!' *Go to 24.*

96

You decided to follow the road to the right because you thought you heard the car speed off to the *left*. You couldn't be absolutely sure about this, though. You were still trying to free yourself from that blanket at the time! Your guess is soon proved correct, though. For the vile couple's car suddenly reappears to your left, speeding past you. Having turned round a bit further up the road, they're obviously making their way back to the loch . . . ***Go to 31***.

97

You chose the *first* parking place because you really couldn't be sure that the light would last until you reached the other two. Indeed, as you hurriedly leap down from the bus, you're not even sure it has lasted *here*. There's now a sombre greyness hanging over and merging with the water, making it seem more sinister than ever. But the monster obviously feels much safer in this gloomy light because the black silhouette of what could be its neck suddenly rises up from the water, only fifty metres in front of you! It's hard to be absolutely sure it is the monster though, and you wonder whether it will be *even harder* to be sure on a photograph. So, do you take one or not?

If yes go to 13
If no go to 65

98

Since you don't have a map, of course, you look to see if there are any yachts in the vicinity of the hotel. There aren't – but that doesn't really prove anything. It's well past the main holiday season now and it's also midweek. So it wouldn't be a busy time for yachts anyway. You now walk a little further along the pebbly shore, keeping your eyes open for anything strange in the water. You give the loch a bit *too* much of your concentration, though. For you suddenly trip on one of the larger pebbles, accidentally pressing your camera's shutter release as you do so!

Delete the top number in your score card's 📷 column. Go next to 75.

99

Yes, this compromise definitely seems the best choice. By not running *too* fast, your footing on this treacherous road is reasonably sure. You would hate to slip and twist your ankle. Or, even worse, damage your camera. On the other hand, by proceeding more quickly than a walk you ensure that you're not left exposed on this lethal road for too long. Indeed, fairly soon, you reach the safety of that last passing place. The irony is, that a few moments later the rain suddenly stops again. You've backtracked all this way for nothing! ***Go to 54.***

100

You should have resisted the temptation. It was just a seal momentarily popping its head out of the water! ***Delete the top number in your score card's 📷 column. Go next to 79.***

101

Having made your way through the trees at the southern side of the hotel, you peer right across the loch to the opposite shore. As you squint at the steep slope there, you shiver excitedly to think that this is exactly the same background as in that famous piece of film! Might you be lucky from this spot too? Your gaze is so intent, though, that it's a while before you move your eyes over to the right. You can just make out a thin dark shape there. Is this merely a fly-fisherman standing in the shallows . . . or could it possibly be the monster's head and neck? The shape starts to shorten. Either the fisherman is wading in deeper – or the monster is starting to dive. If you're going to take a photo, you must do it right now!

If you decide yes   go to 5
If you decide no   go to 142

102

Stepping inside the little church, you do in fact discover the minister there. You quietly approach him and apologise for your interruption. 'Not at all, not at all,' he replies amiably. 'Always delighted to receive visitors to my church!' When you ask him where you might find someone who will row you across the loch, he has to consider for a while. 'Let me see. I think your best bet would probably be Davie MacGregor,' he decides eventually. 'You'll doubtless find him somewhere round the village's little bay. You can't miss him because he always wears a bright orange woolly hat!' ***Go to 57.***

103

As Davie continues on his course, you keep nervously glancing over the side of the boat. How you'd hate to have to swim in that sinister water! Suddenly, though, your attention is diverted by something in the distance, just out from the shore. It looks like the top of a head moving slowly through the water! 'Oh, that's just someone's dog having a paddle,' Davie says, laughing as he glances over his shoulder. A little more of the dark head becomes visible, though, and you're sure it's NOT a dog. Do you quickly take a photo in case it suddenly submerges again?

If yes   go to 129
If no   go to 141

104

Unfortunately, this trail involves an even *steeper* climb to the top, through the fir-trees. Once there, you are only able to lie exhausted on the ground for a while. It is sometime before you catch your breath and are able to take in the panoramic view below. The loch lies dark and mysterious down there . . . but, sadly, those mysteries remain firmly hidden all the time you watch! ***Go to 152***.

105

You now leave the old castle, climbing the short steep footpath back up to the road. You can't help glancing back down at the jagged ruins, though. Perhaps you should watch from there a little longer. It has been the place of so many monster sightings after all. So you decide to stay at the castle another half-hour. But where should you go to make your watch? Should you remain here, high above it . . . descend to about halfway down the footpath . . . or return right to the crumbling stone itself?

Which level will you choose?
  If high above castle   *go to 127*
  If part-way down path *go to 9*
  If down at castle itself *go to 74*

106

Unfortunately, what you thought was the monster, was in fact a leaping salmon! *Delete the top number in your score card's 📷 column. Go next to 79.*

107

About half a mile from the hotel, the road brings you to a tiny village. You decide this is definitely as far as you go along this eastern side of the loch! Your single task now must be to hire someone to ferry you the three quarters of a mile or so to the other side. But how do you find such a person? You'd better enquire somewhere. The village seems to have little more than a tiny grocery shop and a church. You wonder which of these two buildings you should approach . . .

Which will you choose?
If shop   go to 158
If church   go to 39

108

As you now start to climb the ruins of the castle's tower, you recall the most dramatic of the monster photographs taken near here. It shows a huge pair of humps passing right under the castle, almost as long as the tower is high! You're so preoccupied with this mental picture, wondering whether the photo was genuine or not, that you suddenly trip up on one of the stone steps. You hear a heart-breaking *click* from your camera as you just manage to break your fall.

Delete the top number in your score card's 📷 column. Go next to 43.

109

As you continue to follow Angus down to the water's edge, you see that there is absolutely no doubt about his identity. His dog, Blackie, obeys his every command. She certainly wouldn't do this with anyone just *pretending* to be her owner! While Angus is quite genuine, though, he fails to be lucky with the monster a *second* time. You both spend a good quarter of an hour at the spot where he sighted it before – but without seeing a thing. 'Well, thanks for your trouble, anyway,' you say, expressing your gratitude and you bid each other goodbye. ***Go to 136.***

110

Your abductors say nothing during the fast car ride but it doesn't take much to work out exactly who they are. Kate Dupe in the front and Dave Conn holding you down in the back! But where are they taking you? You can just hear the sound of rushing water – so you must be following the road next to the river that leads *due west* from the loch. This is depressingly confirmed when the car suddenly slows down and you are pushed out. The loch is nowhere in sight! Which way should you go to try and make your way back to it again? Walk to the left along this road, to the right – or climb that steep walkers' footpath just opposite to obtain a view?

Which will you choose?
   If follow road to left   go to 15
   If follow road to right   go to 96
   If take footpath   go to 145

111

Well, at least there's no risk of you missing that bus. The trail you followed is so short that you're very soon back at the road! The drawback, though, was that the trail provided hardly any views of the loch at all along the route. The occasional view you did have was no more than a peep between the trees. So if there had been a monster swimming around in the slowly-darkening loch below, you wouldn't have known much about it anyway! ***Go to 148.***

112

You're just wondering if there's any other way you can find out which direction the loch is in, when you suddenly have to leap on to the bank at the side of the road. A speeding car screeches round the corner ahead, seeming to aim right for you! There's just time for you to recognise the occupants before the car disappears. You might have guessed. It's that vile couple again. They obviously turned round a little further up the road so they could make their way back to the loch. At least you now know to turn round yourself. The bad news, though, is that you accidentally wasted an exposure when you leapt out of their way.

Delete the top number in your score card's 📷 column. Go next to 149.

113

As the bus passes the first parking place, you wonder whether you were wise to have chosen the next one instead. The loch's growing darker by the second! Fortunately, though, the second parking place arrives very soon afterwards and you eagerly leap down from the bus. You're hoping that the monster might actually *prefer* to surface in this gloomy light, considering it much safer. And indeed, it looks as if your hopes are to be fulfilled . . . for you suddenly spot a dark shape just under the water! The bus driver helpfully swings his vehicle round, the headlights now shining on the spot. But is it *still* too dark?

If take photo   go to 92
If not   go to 65

114

Having entered the phone box, you carefully sort through your change to see if you have sufficient coins. A long distance call like this to your editor is going to need quite a few! But suddenly there's a tap on the glass behind you and you drop the coins all over the floor in your shock. A middle-aged woman has appeared there and she is impatient to use the phone box herself. Your first reponse is a rather irritated one – but then your eyes suddenly widen with excitement. The woman is wearing exactly the same green scarf as one of those witnesses in that news item! You eagerly open the phone box door to have a word with her . . . ***Go to 132.***

115

Since you don't have a map, you'll just have to hope that you come across a signpost somewhere along the road. Is that one in the far distance? you suddenly wonder after you have turned the next bend. You peer and squint at it for a while before realising that you have a 'telescope' with you of course. The telephoto lens on your camera! Using your camera doesn't prove such a clever idea after all, however. You inadvertently press the shutter release button while you're looking through the view-finder!

Delete the top number in your score card's 📷 column. Go next to 149.

116

You soon realise that you don't need a map to find out if the well is near here. Flipping the postcard over, you read that it's called the Well of St Ignatius and that it's situated fifteen miles west of the loch. There's a bit more detail about the well on the postcard and – so you don't risk missing the bus – you continue clambering up the rocks as you read it. Foolishly, as it turns out. For you suddenly trip, jolting your camera as you fall and wasting a precious photograph.

Delete the top number in your score card's 📷 column. Go next to 148.

117

'Yes, I *am* that same person you saw on the news,' the man confirms modestly as he comes right up to you. 'Angus MacDonald is the name. I glimpsed the monster's two humps when Blackie and I were going for a late afternoon stroll. It was just down the bank here. Come, I'll show you!' As you start to follow the man down through the clearing in the trees, however, you suddenly have a terrible thought . . . ***Go to 156.***

118

It's just an upturned rowing-boat which is being pulled by a long rope! Dave and Kate are obviously behind that bend somewhere! ***Delete the top number in your score card's 📷 column. Go next to 49.***

119

As you continue to watch the loch, you notice that the mist is growing thicker. Soon the dark green slopes of the other side are obscured and so you decide not to waste any more time here. You know that the mists can come and go quite quickly over the loch at this time of year. With any luck, by the time you reach the next clearing along the road, the view will be clearer again! ***Go to 146.***

120

You're just muttering to yourself, complaining that you don't have a map, when the grocer comes running up behind you. 'Oh, I forgot that you wouldn't know where the waterfall is!' he says, panting. 'It's about two miles north of here – ' As he returns to his shop, you make a quick calculation. If the waterfall is about *two miles to the north* and this Davie MacGregor moors his boat *about two miles to the south of it*, then he must row virtually straight across the loch. So you immediately continue hurrying down to the little bay. You're a bit *too* urgent about it, though, failing to notice some damp leaves in your path. As you skid on them, you accidentally hit your camera and take a photo.

Delete the top number in your score card's 📷 column. Go next to 57.

121

You step a little closer to the water in your effort to study the hotel with the flags. Yes, you're sure it *is* a yachting hotel. You have a look through your camera's viewfinder. Suddenly, though, you become more concerned with something else. Your foot. It's soaking wet! In your hurry to leap back from the water, you cause an even bigger disaster. You accidentally press your camera's shutter release button. A few seconds later, you're pulling out a very blurred photograph of your wet shoe!

Delete the top number in your score card's 📷 column. Go next to 75.

122

Unfortunately, you have chosen the *wrong* trail. Its ascent is so gentle that it's a good twenty minutes before you obtain your first view of the loch. Oh well, at least you now know that you must follow the road to the *right*. And your return to that road is via a much steeper and therefore quicker path. You're still annoyed with your choice, though . . . especially when you have to cross a shallow river on your way down. You slip on one of the stepping-stones, accidentally snapping a photograph as you topple!

Delete the top number in your score card's 📷 column. Go next to 149.

123

Unfortunately, you seem to have made the wrong choice. That last passing place is much further back than you remembered! As visibility deteriorates even further, you desperately hope that a speeding car doesn't suddenly appear round the corner, or you could be in great danger. Would it be better to run, you wonder, and cover that remaining distance as quickly as possible? There would be a high risk of slipping on the wet road, though, and injuring yourself... so maybe a slow but sure walk would be the better option. Or perhaps you should go for a compromise between the two and do a gentle jog.

Which will you choose?
If sprint   *go to 35*
If jog   *go to 99*
If walk   *go to 61*

124

Following this trail, you keep hoping that by the time you have reached the next ✈ symbol the trees will have thinned out. But this walk is clearly intended for those who enjoy woods rather than open views! Infuriating, since views are exactly what you need. So it's no disappointment when the trail finally descends back to the shore road again. *Go to 37.*

125

'Hoping to spot the monster, are you?' the farmer calls out. 'That's exactly where I saw it, from the top of that tower! By the way, my name's Duncan MacLean. You might have seen me on the television news last –' But he suddenly breaks off with a gasp. 'Great Scot! There it is again!' he cries. 'Can you see? Quick, move right to the edge of the tower or you'll miss it!' You wonder if this person really is Duncan MacLean, though. Perhaps it's just Dave Conn instead. Those bushy brown sideboards of his might just be stuck on. And should they actually *be* brown, anyway?

If you have circled the NEWSPAPER accessory you may study it now to check if Duncan MacLean really does have brown sideboards. If you haven't, it's your risk whether you trust this man or not:
   If prepared to trust him   go to 46
   If not   go to 89

126

You've been peering straight ahead for some ten minutes when you suddenly make out a dark hump amongst the thrashing waves. Or do you? The storm-swept loch is so turbulent that it might just be a black under-part of the waves. A few seconds later, though, a long neck suddenly rises up in front of the hump. There's no doubt that it's the monster *now*! Your excitement is so great, however, that you momentarily forget about taking a photograph. By the time you've realised this, another lash of rain has swept across your view of the monster. You now can't be sure whether it will be clear enough for a photo.

Do you risk quickly taking one or not?
If yes   go to 150
If no   go to 51

127

It looks like you made the right decision in staying high above the castle. For after a patient watch of the waters beyond it, you suddenly notice a dark shape moving slowly just below the surface. If your viewing angle had been any lower than this, you surely wouldn't have been able to see it. But what is this dark shape under the water? Could it be the monster – or is it simply a large shoal of fish? You suddenly have your answer – for a huge dark grey hump rises up from the loch! It immediately starts to descend again, though, about to disappear. You must think quickly. Is there just time for a photograph?

If you decide yes go to 76
If you decide no   go to 49

128

You cross the road to a steep footpath which climbs up between the trees. A path as steep as this would surely provide a good view of the loch fairly soon. For the moment, though, the path remains very wooded. Then it splits into three. Seeing the symbols painted on the trees, you guess that each branch is the start of a circular nature trail. You wonder which symbol denotes a trail with some views but only of average length. You're worried about missing that bus!

If you have circled the nature trail GUIDE accessory you may consult it now to identify the trail that fits your requirement. If you haven't, you'll have to take a risk in making your choice:
   If trail denoted by 🍀   *go to 88*
   If trail denoted by ♣   *go to 50*
   If trail denoted by 🍀   *go to 111*

129

Well noticed – it was the monster's head you saw! Record this success in the 📷 column of your score card. Also, delete the top number in the 📷 column to show that you have used another photograph. Go next to 141.

130

'I passed a really good viewing place about half a mile back,' the cyclist says as he stops to answer you. 'You'll reach it in about ten minutes or so. It's a clearing with great views of the loch. See you!' As he moves off again, a large plastic wallet slips out of his anorak pocket and falls to the ground. You call after him but his legs are pedalling so fast that he's already out of earshot.

Walking up to the wallet, you see that it is in fact a waterproof cover for a map. The map is still inside and you keep your fingers crossed that it is one for this area. It is!

You are now entitled to use the MAP on the front flap of this book. Circle the M in the 🗺 column of your score card so that you have a reminder of this whenever the map is required. Go next to 146.

131

Since you don't have a map, of course, you console yourself by watching the loch some more. You decide to keep your camera's view-finder fixed on one point, as still as possible, hoping that something exciting will suddenly break through the surface. Is it your imagination, you begin to wonder a bit later, or is there something creeping up behind you? NO, it must just be your imagination. But when you suddenly feel a warm, wet lick on the back of your neck, you nearly jump out of your skin! You turn round just in time to see a deer flee into the trees. So that's all it was! Your amusement is rather short-lived, though. Glancing down at your camera, you see that you accidentally pressed your camera's shutter release and took a photograph when you'd jumped!

Delete the top number in your score card's 📷 column. Go next to 75.

132

'Yes, I am one of those lucky people who witnessed the monster. Wasn't it exciting?' the woman asks you. 'My name's Maggie Gordon, by the way. If you just cross the road with me, I'll show you exactly where I saw it!' You're about to step out of the phone box, however, when you suddenly wonder if this woman could be an impostor. Could she just be that odious Kate Dupe in disguise? You wouldn't be in the least surprised if journalists as unscrupulous as those always carried disguises with them. They are probably an essential part of their professional equipment! So you desperately try to remember what type of hair Maggie Gordon had in that news interview. Was it shoulder-length like this woman's – or close-cropped?

If you have circled the NEWSPAPER accessory you may study it now to find out if this woman is Maggie Gordon, or is really Kate Dupe in disguise. If you have not, it's your risk whether you are prepared to trust her or not:
  If prepared to trust her go to 4
  If not   go to 85

133

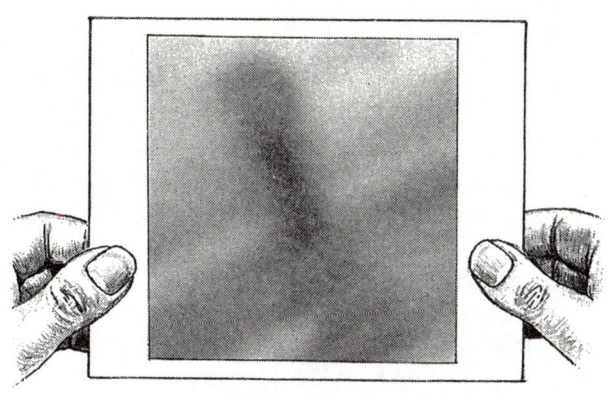

You might know that this grey blur is genuinely the monster – but no one else is likely to think so! So it's worthless, unfortunately. ***Delete the top number in your score card's 📷 column. Go next to 141.***

134

Having returned to the forest track, you start to follow it. You hope that it won't take you too far out of your way. You really can't afford to waste any time. It climbs higher and higher, steeper and steeper, but still you're not above the tree line. All you can see around you are dense woods. Eventually, the track divides into three footpaths. There's a tree stump at the beginning of each footpath, each stump with a symbol painted on it. You guess that these different symbols denote different nature trail walks and you wonder which one you should follow. Your preference is for the least wooded walk so you will be able to see something of the loch at last!

If you have circled the nature trail GUIDE accessory you may consult this now to find out which symbol denotes the least wooded walk. If you haven't, you'll have to take a risk in your choice:
   If trail denoted by ✦   go to 67
   If trail denoted by ✸   go to 8
   If trail denoted by ✹   go to 124

135

Keeping your camera focused on the rapidly disappearing whirlpool, you only hope that you have made the right decision. Perhaps the monster has swum far away by now! But then you hear another splash just beyond the whirlpool. You quickly direct your camera towards this, trying to control your excitement. Was the splash just a leaping salmon, though, or a playful otter? Whatever it is suddenly breaks the surface again, giving you no chance to study it. You realise that if you're going to catch it on photograph, you must snap this very instant. *Will you do so or not?*

If yes   go to 106
If no   go to 79

136

You've walked a mile or so from the telephone box when you reach a small white hotel. 'Foyers Hotel', you read above the door. That name rings a bell. Suddenly, you remember. It was from Foyers Hotel that the famous home movie sequence was shot in the early 1960s. The film that shows something inexplicable speeding across the loch. Something that many experts believe was the monster! This is obviously a spot where you should do some watching yourself. You wonder whether you would be better off remaining at this northern side of the hotel – or continuing to its southern side.

Which side will you choose?
  If northern side *go to 17*
  If southern side *go to 101*

137

'If you let me take your arm,' the friendly woman continues, 'I'll show you the exact spot where I was standing when I saw the monster!' As she reaches out for your arm, however, you're not sure whether you should trust her or not. How do you know that this isn't really Kate Dupe in disguise? True, this woman's a lot stouter than Kate Dupe but that could merely be several layers of clothes and padding in her cheeks. Her hair is different as well – black and curly, but that could easily be a wig, of course. If only you knew what Mrs MacPherson *really* looked like . . .

If you have circled the NEWSPAPER accessory you may study it now to find out if Mrs MacPherson genuinely does have hair which is black and curly. If you haven't picked up the newspaper accessory during the game, it's your risk whether you trust this woman or not:
  If prepared to trust her *go to 90*
  If not   *go to 72*

138

As Davie continues to heave on his oars through the blackish water, you shudder on reminding yourself how deep the loch is – well over two hundred murky metres! 'Ay, it can be quite unsettling if you're not used to it,' your bearded oarsman says, chuckling kindly. 'Now where exactly would you like me to steer towards on the other side? Towards that fallen tree way over to the left, that cluster of boulders way over to the right, or shall I just keep going straight ahead?'

Which direction will you choose?
If towards fallen tree go to 20
If towards boulders go to 42
If straight ahead go to 103

139

First, the rain finally stops. And second, you discover today's local newspaper at the place where the post van had been parked. And the front page is all about the monster sightings! The postman must have unknowingly kicked the paper out while he was stretching his legs. What good fortune! This find will surely help you in your mission.

You are now entitled to use the NEWSPAPER which is shown on the back flap of this book. Circle the N in the 📰 column of your score card so that you have a reminder of this whenever the newspaper is required. Go next to 54.

140

The 'humps' were just two rowing-boats close together! *Delete the top number in your score card's 📷 column. Go next to 68.*

141

You observe no further strange sights on the loch before reaching the opposite shore. Waving Davie goodbye, you scramble up the steep rocky slope to the road. This road is much wider than the one on the other shore, but it's also rather busier, so again you have to be careful as you follow it. You're probably safe enough *now*, but it's likely to be a very different story in a few hours' time when the light starts to fade. So you decide to walk fairly briskly, knowing that you have at least ten miles ahead of you before you're back at the very top of the loch! ***Go to 23***.

142

You now decide to enter the little hotel. But when you try the door, you find that it is locked. It looks as if the hotel might have closed for a period. It is well after the main holiday season, after all. Surely there's *someone* around, though? You wonder whether you should stroll round to the back of the hotel . . . or not lose any more time here and just continue on your way.

What will you decide?
If go round to back *go to 161*
If leave hotel *go to 3*

143
Your anxiety is because there's barely any verge to this single-track road. There's a steep downward slope right next to the loch side of the road and an even steeper upward slope on the mountain side. Although vehicles have been a very rare sight so far, if one does suddenly come along in this blinding rain it could plough right into you! Your best bet is probably to hurry back to that last passing place until visibility becomes a little better.

But it was quite a way. Perhaps you should keep going for the next passing place instead. But that might be an even greater distance. So maybe you should just stay right where you are, after all. No, you decide to keep to your very first choice of action . . . that is to hurry back along the road to the last passing place. ***Go to 123.***

144
You've only gone a little further down the steep bank when you suddenly feel Brother Francis's hand reach out towards your back. It's not to push you, though. It's to warn you . . . because a rock is just about to give way under your foot. If it hadn't been for that hand of his, you could well have slipped all the way down into the water! At last, you both reach the spot where he had been standing before. But your long wait there is completely in vain. 'I'm afraid the place wasn't so lucky this time,' Brother Francis says with a sigh and you finally agree to climb back to the road and go your different ways again. ***Go to 37.***

145

Before it takes you high enough for a good view, the footpath divides into three. Each branch is obviously the start of a circular nature trail because the first tree along their respective routes has an orange symbol painted on it. You wonder which of these three different symbols denotes a trail which is steep both in ascent and descent. Although such a walk will be hard work, you haven't time for a more leisurely one.

If you have circled the nature trail GUIDE accessory, you may consult it now to find out which symbol denotes a walk with a steep ascent and descent. If you haven't, you'll have to take a risk in your choice:
  If you think 🐾 *go to 27*
  If you think 🐿 *go to 47*
  If you think 🌿 *go to 122*

146

You continue walking along the quiet leafy road, pausing to peep through the trees every once in a while. Is it just your wishful thinking – or is the mist over the loch dispersing? And when you reach the next clearing, you have absolutely no doubt about it. It's your clearest view of the other side of the loch yet! The sky is still very grey and threatening but visibility is not at all bad. So you decide to stop here and watch for a while. You can either sit right here at the highest part of the bank, or descend the dozen or so rough steps that lead down to the water's edge!

Which do you choose?
   If stay at higher part   *go to 7*
   If descend steps   *go to 28*

147

The next forest track is only about another 500 metres along the road. It involves a hard climb but, as you make your ascent, panting all the way up, you're sure that the views from the top will be worth it. Before you reach those views, though, the track suddenly divides into three, each path leading in a different direction. You assume that they're nature trails because there are tree stumps at the beginning of each path. One has a 🐿 symbol carved into it, one a 🐕 symbol and the third a 🦆 symbol. You wonder which symbol means that the circular trail has a gentle climb up (so it's not too exhausting) but a steep climb back (so you don't waste too much time).

If you have circled the nature trail GUIDE accessory you may consult it now to find this out. If you haven't, you'll have to take a risk in your choice:
   If trail denoted by 🐿   *go to 14*
   If trail denoted by 🐕   *go to 104*
   If trail denoted by 🦆   *go to 86*

148

Five minutes later, you're boarding the bus and so . . . that's it. No more opportunities to photograph the monster! As you take a seat on the small, empty bus, though, you notice that there's still just a little light left in the sky. It's as if this last trace stubbornly refuses to disappear. Maybe with a long exposure, then, you *could* still obtain one last photograph . . . ***Go to 11.***

149

You're at last approaching the loch again – but it's now considerably darker. In the hour and a half or so it has taken you to make your way back there, the sun has started to set over the water. You estimate that you now have not much more than an hour of decent light left for taking photographs! That must have been exactly what Dave and Kate had intended, of course, when they forcefully took you all those miles out of your way. Well, you're determined not to let that wasted time be a hindrance to your assignment. You hurry right up to the edge of the loch to watch. Do you look to the left, the right or straight ahead?

If to left	***go to 52***
If to right	***go to 93***
If straight ahead	***go to 30***

150

Well risked. The monster is just clear enough! Record this success in the 🎞 column of your score card. Also, delete the top number in the 📷 column. Go next to 51.

151

'You're a newspaper photographer, aren't you?' the man continues genially. 'I can see that from your professional-looking camera. May I have a quick look at it? I'm a bit of a photographer myself, although only an amateur, of course. In return, I'll show you where I sighted the monster. I'm sure that's what you've come to Loch Ness for!' But as he advances towards you and your precious camera, you discreetly protect it with your hand. 'No, actually I'm a calendar photographer, really only interested in scenery,' you lie. 'And I really must be going, I'm afraid. I'm falling badly behind schedule!' ***Go to 107.***

152

This trail is equally steep in its descent towards the road. But you don't mind until it becomes so steep that you have to break into a helpless run through the trees. As the road approaches, the only way you can stop yourself is by deliberately colliding into one of the trees. You knock your camera's shutter release button as you do so!

Delete the top number in your score card's 📷 column. Go next to 37.

153

Having scrambled down the short but steep slope to the water's edge, you notice a rowing-boat coming towards you. 'Good evening to ye,' the man in the boat calls out. He's wearing a dark blue fisherman's hat, brown side-whiskers sprouting out from underneath. He also has a scar under one eye. 'Ye'll be watching for the monster, nae doubt?' he asks. 'Jump in and I'll row you to exactly the spot where I myself, Jamie MacTavish, sighted it the other day!' You gratefully accept this offer. But as he starts to row you out into the slowly-darkening loch, you wonder if this man really is Jamie MacTavish.

If you have circled the NEWSPAPER accessory you may study it now to check if Jamie MacTavish fits this man's description. If you haven't, it's your risk whether you trust him or not:
  If trust him   go to 95
  If not   go to 32

154

Since you don't have a map to use, you seem to have no choice but to continue walking. You calculate that you must have covered at least ten miles by now. If you remember correctly, the loch is some *twenty-two* miles in length. So you decide one more mile to take you halfway and then you'd better start thinking about exploring the other side of the loch. That's always assuming, of course, that you're able to find someone to row you across! ***Go to 107.***

155

As you're exploring the castle's crumbling walls, you suddenly notice that you're not alone. A stoutish woman in a green scarf has appeared. She scrambles towards you. 'Hello there, I'm Mrs MacPherson,' she says, panting. 'I come here for a short walk every day. Generally, it's just me and the deserted ruins but you'll never guess what I spotted from here yesterday – a long dinosaur-like neck sticking out of the water!' ***Go to 137.***

Your terrible thought is that *this could be Dave Conn in disguise*! You could easily imagine that unscrupulous couple having various disguises in their luggage – probably an essential part of their professional equipment! Dave Conn certainly didn't have a dog with him at the airport, of course . . . but who said this was this man's dog anyway? She might have just wandered here from one of the nearby farms. Oh, if only you could remember a bit more about Angus MacDonald's appearance so you could prove Dave had got part of his disguise wrong! Was his hair really black and straight like this man's for instance? Or was it black and *curly*!

If you have circled the NEWSPAPER accessory, you may study this now to find out if Angus MacDonald does have straight black hair. If you haven't, it's your risk whether you trust him or not:

If trust him   go to 109
If not   go to 64

157

You now enter the rather eerie tower and start to climb the steps towards the top. You're about halfway up when you suddenly hear a strange raucous cry through one of the open stone windows. Is this the *monster's* cry? Is it currently swimming right past where the castle juts out? No, there's a much simpler explanation. For a large crow suddenly flies in through the window. But it's still enough to give you a bit of a shock . . . and to make you accidentally take a photo!

Delete the top number in your score card's 📷 column. Go next to 43.

158

'Oh, the man you'll be wanting is Davie MacGregor,' the bespectacled grocer informs you when you have entered his shop. 'Yes, Davie's your man all right. He rows across the loch most afternoons, mooring about two miles south of the waterfall on the other side. You'll find him and his boat down by the wee bay, a few hundred metres from here. You'll know him by his bright orange woolly hat. Never takes it off, he doesn't. Even when he's asleep, they say!' ***Go to 6.***

159

You jump as you suddenly hear someone panting behind you. 'Phew, the bus hasn't come yet, then?' asks a woman with short black hair. After she has recovered her breath, she tells you that her name is Mrs Campbell. 'And you'll never guess what I saw when I was walking to this bus stop yesterday,' she chatters. 'The monster! I'll show you the exact spot if you like. It was just a few metres back from here.' Knowing that this is your very last chance of a photograph, you eagerly start to follow Mrs Campbell. But then you wonder if she's really Kate Dupe in disguise . . .

If you have circled the NEWSPAPER accessory you may study it now to check if Mrs Campbell fits this description. If you haven't, it's your risk whether you trust her or not:

If prepared to trust her   *go to 81*
If not   *go to 59*

160

You're wondering if you've done the right thing in staying where you are. You could have got back to the last passing place by now and you might have reached the next passing place even more quickly! If only there were more of a verge by the road to stand back on when a vehicle passed – but there's a virtually sheer slope on the loch side and a *totally* sheer slope on the mountain side. It could be very dangerous for you in this driving rain. Fortunately, though, still no vehicle appears and it's not much longer now before the rain finally subsides. ***Go to 54.***

161

'Hello, can I help you?' a friendly Scottish voice asks as you wander round to the back of the hotel. It belongs to a lean-faced man with straight black hair. 'My name's Jock Reid,' he adds. 'I look after the hotel.' You feel an immediate excitement on hearing this name. Jock Reid was one of the witnesses filmed on that news item! Or could this just be Dave Conn in a wig? you start to wonder with a sudden shiver. How can you be sure? You really need to study a photo of Jock Reid . . .

If you have circled the NEWSPAPER accessory, you may study it now to find out if this really is Jock Reid. If you have not, it's your risk whether you trust him or not:

   If trust him   go to 83
   If not   go to 151

162

Stepping into this clearing, you peer down the long sloping bank. There's a small wooden hut part of the way down, perched some five metres above the water. The large open window at the front, directly overlooking the loch, makes you guess that it's probably a monster-observation hut! Or, at least, *used* to be a monster-observation hut . . . because it's now very dilapidated. You wonder whether you should climb down there and have a look inside. Perhaps you'll find some fascinating notes about the monster. Or would you just be wasting your time? What will you decide?

If investigate hut   go to 38
If give it a miss   go to 119

163

Soon after passing the next forest track, you spot a monk, coming towards you along the road. He's wearing a brown habit and has slightly lighter brown curly hair. 'Hoping to photograph the monster, are you?' he asks genially. 'If you like, I'll take you to the very spot where *I* witnessed it. It's just back along this road a bit, part way down the bank. My name's Brother Francis, by the way. I live in the abbey at the very south of the loch.' You're grateful for this assistance but as the monk directs you down the steep treacherous bank, you start to become suspicious of him. Is this really just Dave Conn, intending to give you a sudden push in the back?

If you have circled the NEWSPAPER accessory you may study it now to check if Brother Francis really does look like this. If you haven't, it's your risk whether you trust him or not:
   If prepared to trust him   go to 144
   If not   go to 21

Collect all four titles in this series:

And have you also read Stephen Thraves' Super Adventure Game Books with separate cards and special dice?